The Fauna Preservation Society
1903 - 1978

The Penitent Butchers

Richard Fitter

Sir Peter Scott

Collins · St James Place, London

First published 1978
© Fauna Preservation Society 1978
ISBN 0 00 219416 3 Collins Edition
ISBN 0 00 259418 8 Fauna Preservation Society Edition
Designed and Printed by Print + Design, Reading

Contents

Acknowledgments

The author is grateful to the following, who read all or part of the manuscript, but is of course responsible for any remaining errors: Phyllis Barclay-Smith, Lt. Col. C.L. Boyle, John A. Burton, Sir Hugh Elliott and Maisie Fitter. Thanks are due also to those who supplied various pieces of information: The Earl of Cranbrook, G.T. Corley Smith, Mrs. Stanley Flower, Vivien Gledhill, Kay Gordon, Janet Kear, David Ride, Tim Sands, Jane Thornback and Col. Jack Vincent. A special word of thanks to our Chairman, Sir Peter Scott, who took time out of his very busy schedule to make the excellent drawings that adorn these pages, and to Lt. Col. C.L. Boyle, who made numerous abstracts from the society's early journals, and to the House of Collins, whose late Chairman, Sir William Collins, was an active member of the FPS Council.

R.F., June 1978

4

1 | The FPS Today

The Fauna Preservation Society celebrates its 75th anniversary in December 1978. Founded in 1903 as the Society for the Preservation of the Wild Fauna of the Empire, it was the first society in the world to be specifically interested in wildlife conservation overseas. It is also the second oldest British conservation society. Its primary object is to ensure that natural wildlife populations and their habitats are maintained at optimum levels throughout the world, with particular emphasis on species in danger of extinction. To this end it seeks:

1. Conservation of habitats for wildlife, especially by national parks and other reserves;
2. Legislation, at national, regional and local levels and its enforcement;
3. Education for all ages, on the importance of wildlife conservation for human welfare; and
4. Captive breeding of endangered species with a view to their ultimate release in the wild.

The Society works closely with other conservation bodies, both national and international. Its panel of 108 honorary overseas consultants in 70 different countries enables it to keep informed about current problems on a world-wide basis.

The Society's journal ORYX was known until 1950 as the *Journal of the Society for the Preservation of the Fauna of the Empire*. Today it is the leading journal in its field and is in many ways unique. Edited since 1964 by Maisie Fitter and published three times a year, it covers a wide range of conservation news from all parts of the world combined with original illustrated articles on a popular scientific level with editorial notes, and book reviews. It is an invaluable source of information for all members, particularly those overseas, who form one-third of the FPS membership. It is also to be found in libraries throughout the world.

The Oryx 100% Fund gives small grants of up to £500 to urgent conservation projects; in the six years since it was launched it has grant-aided 151 projects dealing with more than 75 endangered species in 50 countries to a total of £40,350.

Other important current activities are support for two key IUCN activities, the Red Data Book for Mammals (see p 00), whose compiler is housed in the Society's offices, and the IUCN TRAFFIC Group on the international wildlife trade (see p 00), which was until recently also housed by the Society. Within the last year FPS has also, through the press, raised small funds on behalf of Grevy's zebra and the mountain gorilla, and is administering a grant from the Vincent Wildlife Trust for a survey of rivers in England for suitable areas to establish otter havens, two of which have already been set up. FPS was one of the pioneers of overseas wildlife tours. These are planned to indicate the value of wildlife tourism to the countries concerned, at the same time as enabling members to see some of the wildlife they are helping to conserve and some of the problems involved. Since 1966 Oryx Tours have visited East Africa, the Galapagos Islands, India, Madagascar, Mauritius, Rwanda, Zaire, Botswana and Zambia.

At its 75th Anniversary the FPS expresses its warmest thanks to the Zoological Society of London, which has given the Society house room, until very recently free of any charge, almost from the beginning. The records of neither Society reveal exactly when this very happy arrangement began. The Zoological Society of London can justly claim that alongside its excellent record in breeding endangered species, its long-term support of the Fauna Preservation Society is a major contribution to the cause of wildlife conservation, and enables it to take its place alongside such notable conservationist zoos as Frankfurt, Jersey, New York and San Diego.

2 | *How FPS Began*

Like man himself, international wildlife conservation began in Africa. How right was the old Greek proverb, quoted by Pliny, that new ideas are always coming out of Africa, *ex Africa semper aliquid novi!* Already in 1900, Britain, Germany, Spain, the Congo (then an independent nation under King Leopold of the Belgians), France, Italy and Portugal, had signed in London a Convention for the Preservation of Animals, Birds and Fish in Africa. The British plenipotentiaries included the Earl of Hopetoun, grandfather of the present Marquess of Linlithgow and Ray Lankester, the well known zoologist, then Director of the Natural History Department of the British Museum. This Convention had been necessitated by the unbridled hunting of game, by Europeans. Even then people were predicting the extinction of wild game in Africa; the blaaubok and the quagga had already gone. Nobody was interested in non-game animals, which it was presumed were in no danger because nobody wanted to hunt them. And of course habitat destruction, so rife in the Mediterranean, had hardly begun in Africa south of the Sahara.

So when in early 1903 naturalists in Britain heard alarming rumours that the authorities in the Sudan were about to abandon the excellent game reserve north of the Sobat river, a tributary of the White Nile, and substitute an inferior area to the south of it, many people were already alerted to the potential dangers of such a move. The man who took action was Edward North Buxton, Verderer of Epping Forest, who organised a letter to Lord Cromer, Governor-General of the Sudan, arguing against it; after much correspondence Cromer agreed.

Buxton's signatories were headed by the Duke and Duchess of Bedford, who at Woburn had already started on the process of saving Père David's deer, and included such notable naturalists as Lord Avebury, Abel Chapman, Sir Edward Grey, Sir Harry Johnston, Ray Lankester, Richard Lydekker, John G. Millais, Philip Lutley Sclater, Frederick Selous, and Oldfield Thomas. So the Fauna Preservation Society had a star-studded caste from the start, for the indefatigable Buxton, seeing he was on to a good thing, proceeded to organise his bunch of notables, along with others, as the Society for the Preservation of the Wild Fauna of the Empire, which was formally launched on December 11, 1903. The new society saw itself as "a modest and unpretentious group of gentlemen of wide experience of the outposts of Empire and a common enthusiasm for the preservation from destruction of many of its fauna". At the end of its first year it was congratulating itself on having 70 ordinary and 30 honorary members, and its Vice-Presidents were of great eminence: Lords Cromer, Grey, Milner, Curzon of Kedleston and Minto, every one of them pillars of the Establishment. The honorary members included President Theodore Roosevelt of the United States, Lord Kitchener of Khartoum, and the Rt. Hon. Alfred Lyttelton, Secretary of State for the Colonies. Its aims were to encourage the protection of the wild fauna in all British possessions from "appalling destruction", and it appealed to colonial administrators to help by reporting on the status and protection of species in their area. Since the Empire at that time covered about a quarter of the surface of the globe, it was a fair start on internationalising the infant wildlife conservation movement. And since it began, like domestic wildlife protection, as an effort to preserve game animals, sportsmen can reasonably claim to have been in the forefront of the movement even if non-sportsmen have always found it hard to understand their ambivalent claim to be "real lovers of nature".

Indeed quite soon the founders of the SPWFE began to be lampooned as "penitent butchers", and a somewhat pained note appeared in the fourth issue of the Society's *Journal* disclaiming the very idea that "we are ... men who, having in earlier days taken their fill of big-game slaughter and the delights of the chase in wild, outlying parts of the earth, now, being smitten with remorse, and having reached a less strenuous term of life, think to condone our earlier bloodthirstiness by advocating the preservation of what we formerly chased or killed". So right from the beginning, conservationists were accused of being, in the modern jargon, elitists, who try to kick down the ladder behind them so that nobody else can follow.

After World War 1 the SPWFE dropped the "Wild", to become the Society for the Preservation of the Fauna of the Empire, and in 1950 it contracted its name still further to the Fauna Preservation Society and renamed its journal Oryx. For much of its life it has been familiarly dubbed "the Fauna".

Historically, wildlife protection has always begun as an attempt to preserve game animals from overshooting or overhunting, and has only later developed into a desire to preserve wild creatures for their own sakes. This was so, for instance, in England, which had game laws of a kind in the Middle Ages, but where legislative action to protect other species did not come till 1869, with the act to preserve seabirds from wanton shooting. Not till a few years after the (not yet Royal) Society for the Protection of Birds was founded in 1889 did the domestic movement to protect wildlife really get under way. The international wildlife movement was correspondingly slow to move from the protection of game animals to the protection of wildlife generally, and the idea of conserving whole ecosystems did not gain general acceptance till well after World War II.

Even before 1914 there was another stirring in the direction of international nature conservation, in Switzerland, but here Paul Sarasin was frustrated by the outbreak of war. However, his initiative ultimately led, just before World War II, to the setting up, at the instance of the Dutchman Pieter van Tienhoven, of the International Office for the Protection of Nature in Brussels. These two strands combined after the war into an initiative taken by the Schweizerbund für Naturschutz in 1946. By this time the Society for the Preservation of the Fauna of the Empire was rapidly catching up with events. It played its part in the formation of the International Union for the Protection of Nature (IUPN) at Fontainebleau, France, in 1948, and two years later signified its own new wider interests by changing its name to the Fauna Preservation Society and that of its Journal, prophetically, to Oryx. In 1956 IUPN itself shook off the remnant of pre-war attitudes when, as a condition of American support, it changed its name to the International Union for Conservation of Nature and Natural Resources (IUCN). The stage was now set for the world-wide spread of environmental and wildlife conservationist attitudes, with only one more major actor still to appear on the stage, the World Wildlife Fund in 1961, arising out of the urgent need to raise funds to run IUCN.

Throughout this period FPS has been closely connected with both IUCN and WWF. Its close interest in the problem of endangered species has been reflected in the fact that for some twenty years the Chairman of IUCN's Survival Service Commission has been a high Officer of the FPS, and so has the Chairman of WWF's International Trustees. Moreover, the Hon. Secretary of the FPS has been a leading member of the SSC throughout this period, and many FPS Council and ordinary members have been chairmen of SSC Specialist Groups. FPS also has an official representative on SSC, currently the Editor of *Oryx*, Maisie Fitter.

Today, while some wild animals and plants still have to be protected from direct human depredation — the great whales, for instance, and the many animals involved in the pet and curio trades — by far the greatest threat to the world's wildlife comes from habitat destruction. Tropical rain forests, for example, are being felled, for short-term gains, at a rate which ensures that they will almost all be gone by the end of the century. By that time also it seems unlikely that there will be any substantial natural ecosystems outside national parks and other protected areas throughout the tropics. Perhaps only parts of the northern hemisphere taiga and tundra, the Antarctic and a few very remote oceanic islands will by the year 2000 remain in anything approaching their pristine condition. At the time of writing, although the international wildlife conservation movement is moving in the right direction, it is moving so slowly that it cannot possibly rectify this imbalance unaided. A sharp change of gear is urgent if our present aims are to be achieved. Ultimately governments will have to be more deeply involved, and this means that politicians must be made to realise that people actually want their environment preserved, not destroyed. In the hope of stimulating this, the Fauna Preservation Society offers the present analysis of what has been happening during the past three-quarters of a century. The remaining chapters will survey some of the problems we have grappled with so far, starting with the creation of national parks, which, in a sense is where we came in.

3 Holy Place to Hunting Reserve

Artemis, the Greek goddess also known as Diana of the Ephesians, symbolises the origins of wildlife conservation. As earth goddess and virgin huntress she embodied the twin strands that made up the embryo conservation movement down to the end of the 19th century. Many primitive peoples had strong religious feelings towards trees, and sacred groves, as readers of *The Golden Bough* will remember,

11

were widespread. Even today, in many parts of Asia, the only sanctuaries for wildlife in a heavily cultivated countryside are these sacred groves, sometimes surrounding a temple, sometimes merely preserved by religious feeling or even superstition. One of the most famous is the Sarnath deer park near Benares on the River Ganges in northern India, where Gautama Buddha preached some 2,500 years ago. Deer parks were also a feature of ancient China, and it was the Imperial Hunting Park at Peking that preserved Père David's deer from extinction. Not only trees but animals too can be most effectively protected by a belief that bad luck will befall the man who destroys them. On the other hand an unfortunate creature such as the aye-aye, a unique lemur in Madagascar which is reputed to bring bad luck to anyone who sees it, is well started on the road to extinction. Maybe this is why the giant aye-aye, known only from fossilised remains, perished in the same island.

Primitive peoples also had ambivalent attitudes towards the animals they hunted, as we know from cave paintings as far back as the Old Stone Age. Like the sportsmen of today, they loved them as a vital source of food and fertility magic, but had to kill them to acquire these benefits. So the need to preserve stocks of animals to hunt became the first non-religious motive for wildlife conservation, a motive that came into play only after the original abundance of wild animals began to dwindle. That the lesson took some learning is indicated by the probability that many large animals were exterminated by early man in the Americas. Chieftains in many parts of the world are known to have set aside hunting reserves; one of the best known, which still survives, is the New Forest in southern England, created 900 years ago by William the Conqueror, the man who "loved the tall deer as if he were their father". By the end of the Middle Ages the hunting reserve was a well recognised technique for preserving stocks of game, allied with the game laws, which also have a long history.

William the Conqueror punished deer poachers by cutting off their hands; his successors executed them. Nevertheless poaching continued to be widely practised in England by all classes alongside legal hunting, and the game laws continued to be harsher than common sense would suggest right down to the present day. This severity often led to a corresponding violence from poachers, as is graphically illustrated by Richard Jefferies in The Gamekeeper at Home (1878) and The Amateur Poacher (1879). Today the game species form a relatively small part of the wildlife we try to conserve, and laws that protect partridges and pheasants more severely than owls and songbirds seem out of place in the climate of late 20th-century Europe. In many parts of the tropics poaching in game reserves and other protected areas still represents a problem, which is tackled with varying effectiveness by the governments in question. In East Africa heavily armed gangs of poachers have recently fought pitched battles with game rangers, several of whom have been killed. If the killing of animals for personal consumption could somehow be separated from killing for commercial sale, many conservationists would be happy to allow local people who have traditionally hunted for subsistence to continue to do so, even in national parks. After all, most wild stocks have withstood this sort of subsistence hunting for centuries, and are adapted to the small annual harvest which it represents.

Until little more than a century ago the need to set aside reserves where the shooting of game could be controlled remained the sole motive for wildlife protection by public authorities and by any but the most eccentric landowners. The British colonial authorities lost little time in creating such reserves in East Africa and the Sudan at the end of the 19th century, because one of the few amenities that could be offered to soldiers (officers only, of course) and administrators marooned in darkest Africa — then rapidly becoming lit up — was shooting big game, and even then it was apparent that game in the more easily accessible areas could soon be shot out. The oldest proclaimed game reserves· in Africa are Hluhluwe, St. Lucia and Umfolozi in Natal, set up in April 1897. As we have seen, it was concern about a reserve in the southern Sudan that led to the formation of the Society for the Preservation of the Wild Fauna of the Empire in 1903.

These game reserves persist right down to the present day in many African countries, and have often developed into means of enabling visiting sportsmen to shoot under conditions that bring substantial revenue and foreign exchange to the local treasuries, as well as employment to local people. Only in 1977 did the Government of Kenya ban this hunting by foreign sportsmen, officially to help stamp out poaching, though many people believe it may actually encourage it. Certainly poaching has not been stopped in Tanzania, which banned sport hunting in 1973. Pressure to be allowed to shoot for trophies is still very strong in the United States and in parts of Europe, but nowadays the hunting organisations all feel bound to pay at least lip service to the need for conservation. To do it justice, the International Council for Wildlife and Game Preservation does appear genuinely to believe in this need, and to wish to collaborate fully with the international wildlife conservation movement. But some North American societies still contrive to give the impression that success in the chase is more important than survival of the species. Pictures of proud hunters beside slumped animal corpses have an increasingly dated look.

So far we have only discussed the restrictionist aspects of the game preservers' contribution to wildlife conservation, but there are more positive actions, such as the reintroduction of depleted or lost species, and the creation of new habitat. Reintroduction of red deer, grey partridge, brown trout and other well known game animals has been going on in Britain for at least three hundred years, for as early as 1673 King Charles II was releasing French or red-legged partridges in his parks at Richmond and Windsor, to supplement the native grey partridge stock which he and his courtiers had evidently overshot. More recently bodies such as Ducks Unlimited in North America and the Wildfowlers' Association in Britain have tackled both the large-scale release of ducks and geese to supplement depleted stocks, and the creation of new wetland habitat. Of these two, habitat creation is far the more valuable, for the depleted stocks are usually the fault of the sportsmen but the depleted habitat is mostly beyond their control. Moreover there are great dangers in introducing new species for sporting purposes. Untold damage has been done to native ecosystems and their associated fauna by, for instance, introduced red deer in New Zealand and introduced goats in Hawaii. In both countries the sporting interests resist any curtailing of the area occupied by the alien sporting animals in the interests of the native fauna and flora, and this is particularly disastrous in Hawaii, which, when it was discovered by Captain Cook, was an even finer evolutionary laboratory than the Galapagos Islands are today.

Generally speaking, however, the more realistic approach of the modern sportsmen brings him into increasing accord with the wildlife conservationist, in an alliance which has been especially constructive and successful as between the Wildfowlers' Association and the former Nature Conservancy in Britain. FPS has joined in a similar meeting of minds between the sporting bodies and the conservation societies concerned with mammals. In 1965 it promoted a symposium on mammal predators. Out of this grew the Mammals Committee, which meets regularly at the House of Commons and has produced a useful booklet on *Predatory Mammals in Britain*, a code of practice for their management. A similar booklet on predatory birds, has been issued, in conjunction with the bird protection societies. The FPS also joined with other conservation and sporting bodies to promote the Deer Act, 1963, which was the first conservation law, in the modern sense, for wild deer in England and Wales, and supported both the Badgers Act 1973 and the Conservation of Wild Creatures and Wild Plants Act, 1975. In 1977 it joined with other conservation bodies in successfully pressing the Government to protect the otter under the latter Act.

4 | National Parks and Emperor Nero

Once the purely religious motive for setting aside inviolate areas had petered out, as it did in the west a long time ago, the modern idea of preserving landscape or animals for their own sake was very slow to grow. In medieval Europe there was little sign of any conservation of wildlife for aesthetic reasons, and the few indications we have, such as St Columba and the eider ducks on Lindisfarne, or St Hugh of Lincoln with his swans, and most notably the life and work of St Francis of Assisi, show that partiality to animals was regarded as an amiable eccentricity, allowable in a saint, but no part of the everyday world. Indeed in 18th-century England the interest of Lady Glanville in butterflies was regarded as so sure a mark of mental imbalance that her will was disputed on that ground. "My friends solemnly regarded me as a madman", John James Audubon confided to his journal of 1823. And when a few years later Charles Waterton not only refused to allow the keepers on his Yorkshire estate to shoot owls but actually put up nest-boxes for starlings, he scandalised the local gentry, and dumbfounded his gamekeepers.

Examples of anything that can be regarded as a genuine wildlife sanctuary before the mid-19th century are very few. Perhaps the earliest of all was the Haagse Bos (the Wood of the Hague), set aside by the Prince of Orange and the States of Holland in 1576. One of Charles Waterton's main claims to the label of eccentricity which made him so indignant was to have walled in Walton Park in 1826, to make a bird sanctuary. The first protected area in what is now Czechoslovakia was set aside as early as 1838. In 1858 a group of painters, for aesthetic reasons, succeeded in having a portion of the Forest of Fontainebleau, near Paris, legally protected. Not till the celebrated campfire discussion in a remote part of Wyoming stimulated the United States Congress to create the Yellowstone National Park in 1872 was the modern movement truly launched. Canada followed with the Banff National Park in 1887, and five years later President Kruger of the Transvaal, one of the handful of political leaders who can claim real credit for understanding and promoting wildlife conservation, protected the Sabie Game Reserve in the same way. The Belair National Park in South Australia was founded in 1891, and the Tongarivo National Park in New Zealand in 1894. In Britain the National Trust was launched in 1895 and at once began to acquire land in the Lake District, but for general amenity rather than wildlife protection. In 1898 Mexico took steps to protect an important forest area and in Kenya the Ukamba Game Reserve, set up in 1899, included the present Amboseli National Park. In 1907 the SPWFE's *Journal* refers to "the sanctuaries which it is one of the aims of the Society to establish throughout the Empire ere it be too late."

So at the beginning of the 20th century the national park movement was in its veriest infancy, and little more happened until after the First World War, despite the strong support of President Theodore Roosevelt, another of the pioneer statesmen of the movement, whose thoughts and pronouncements have a surprisingly modern ring. As early as 1907 he was declaring that "the conservation of our natural resources and their proper use constitute the fundamental problem which underlies almost every other problem of our national life", and in the following year he sent his congratulations to the SPWFE. But not for the first or last time the Congress took little notice of the President's wishes. However in the 1920s the national parks movement got its second wind. In 1919 an important seed had been sown at another Yellowstone campfire when three leading conservationists discussed with King Albert of the Belgians how national parks could be used not only to preserve beautiful landscapes and endangered animals, but also to promote systematic scientific study of what we now call ecosystems. The three conservationists were John C. Merriam, grandfather of Lee Merriam Talbot, Fairfield Osborn of the New York Zoological Society and Victor van Straelen of Belgium, the two latter, along with Lee M. Talbot, later becoming Vice-Presidents of the FPS. In 1925 in what is now Zaire, King Albert created the Gorilla Sanctuary which became first the Parc National Albert and later the Virunga National Park, named after the famous range of volcanoes on its boundary. In the later 1930s Belgium followed this up with three more national parks, one of which, the Parc des Volcans in Rwanda, bordered on the Albert Park and so protected almost the whole range of the rare mountain gorilla. In 1929 we find the Baron de Cartier de Marchienne, longtime Belgian Ambassador in London between the wars, urging the SPFE to secure the protection of the remaining fragment of gorilla territory in the Virunga Volcanoes, which lay in Uganda. This was eventually achieved, but not until 1964.

Perhaps stimulated by the activity of the Belgians, Col. Stevenson-Hamilton, at that time Secretary of the SPFE, managed to secure, in 1926, the conversion of Kruger's Sabie Game Reserve into the Kruger National Park in the Transvaal. The two London Conferences for the Protection of African Fauna and Flora in 1933 and 1938, in which leading members of the SPFE played an active part, resulted in a convention, which gave a great fillip to the national park movement, and was responsible, for instance, for the creation of the Hailey (now Corbett) National Park in India and the Gorongosa Strict Nature Reserve in Mozambique, both in 1935. In Asia the Netherlands had set up an important group of nature reserves in what is now Indonesia as early as 1919, and Japan played a leading role, with a dozen parks established in the mid 1930s under the inspiration of Tuyoshi Tamura. Another vital series of strict nature reserves were created in Madagascar in 1927, which, despite setbacks, have helped to preserve the unique Malagasy fauna.

But the inter-war years were not auspicious for a real take-off of the movement, and it was not until the years surrounding 1953, when a similar conference, also largely masterminded by FPS worthies, was held at Bukavu in the still Belgian Congo, that the great flowering of the national park movement outside the United States took place. Those years saw the creation of the great constellation of East African national parks: Nairobi and Tsavo in Kenya (1946 and 1948), Kafue in Northern (now Zambia) and Wankie in Southern Rhodesia (1950), Serengeti in Tanganyika (now Tanzania) (1951) and Murchison Falls (now Kabalega) and Queen Elizabeth (now Rwenzori) in Uganda (1952). By this time, IUCN had come into being, and its International Commission on National Parks, under the leadership of Harold J. Coolidge of the United States and Jean-Paul Harroy of Belgium, has been the leading influence in this field for the past twenty years. It promoted two World Conferences on National Parks, the first at Seattle in 1962 and the second at the Yellowstone and Grand Teton National Parks in 1972 in conjunction with the Yellowstone centenary celebrations. IUCN also produces the *United Nations List of National Parks and Equivalent Reserves*, originally in collaboration with the UN Economic and Social Council and later at the specific request of the UN Secretary-General. The FPS continued to support the national parks movement generally, and to interest itself in certain individual cases, most notably the Serengeti National Park. In 1956 this was threatened with severe truncation by the British trusteeship administration. The FPS financed a survey by the eminent ecologist, W.H. Pearsall FRS, whose report showed that the whole area was a single ecosystem that must be preserved intact for the sake of the migrations of the vast herds of wildebeest, zebras and other plains game, and secured the retention of the Park as a single unit. The only exception was the Ngorongoro Crater, for which a special conservation unit was created. This also has stood the test of time.

Conservationists have for so long pinned their faith in national parks and nature reserves as the prime means of saving not only endangered species, but wildlife as a whole, that it seems heretical to suggest that the idea is imperfect in any way. But today habitat destruction is proceeding at such a pace that the creation of reserves, however effective twenty or thirty years ago, is now plainly inadequate. Most national parks and nature reserves are much too small — even the Serengeti, with its 1,295,000 ha, does not comprise the whole ecosystem used by the plains game, and the widespread use of agricultural fertilisers means that, strictly speaking, whole river basins ought to be conserved if the waters are to be protected from contamination by nitrates and phosphates. This is a problem world conservationists have scarcely begun to face up to; some are still arguing about exactly how a national park should be defined. The parallel with the Emperor Nero is uncomfortably close. Conservationists simply must find some way of conserving a substantial proportion of the world's remaining unspoiled ecosystems without waiting to see exactly how these areas are going to be named, administered or used.

5 | *How IUCN and WWF Began*

The strands of the conservation movement that led to the eventual formation of IUCN and WWF derived from the activities of three men before World War I, the Swiss Paul Sarasin, the Dutchman Pieter van Tienhoven and the Belgian Victor van Straelen. Sarasin's great achievement was the formation in 1914 of the Swiss National Park in the Engadin. Most European countries, including also Poland, Russia and Sweden, were making their first moves towards setting aside nature reserves or national parks in this decade, but the war naturally put a stop to all progress, even in the neutral countries, and Sarasin's attempts to get an international movement going stalled like everything else. In the 1920s progress was rather slow, although Italy did create the Gran Paradiso National Park above Aosta in 1922. There was an International Congress for the Protection of Nature in Paris in 1931, attended by the SPFE President, the Earl of Onslow, as an official British Government delegate, and by Captain Keith Caldwell and SPFE Secretary C.W. Hobley as delegates of the Society itself. Doubtless because of the Great Depression, then at its height, this conference had singularly little impact. At this time, the SPFE was still declaring that its main object was to ensure that no more species of

19

wild animals should be exterminated within the British Empire. Its three methods of achieving this were to influence public opinion, to promote national parks and to enforce game laws. It was eventually van Tienhoven who picked up the threads, and succeeded in founding the International Office for the Protection of Nature (IOPN) in Brussels in 1938, only to be frustrated again, by World War II.

However, in 1946 the Swiss, relatively unscathed by the war, revived the twice stalled international movement, and found a ready echo in the two Low Countries veterans, van Tienhoven and van Straelen. By a fortunate chance the Wild Life Conservation Special Committee had just been set up by the British Government as part of its post-war reconstruction effort, with Julian Huxley as Chairman. This committee sent a group of its members (including the present writer as its Secretary) to inspect the Swiss National Park in 1946, and the opportunity was taken by the Schweizerbund für Naturschutz to hold an embryo international wildlife conservation conference. The party that eventually toured the Swiss National Park also had representatives from France, Belgium and the Netherlands (van Tienhoven himself), and at a series of meetings in Basle, Zernez and Brunnen, the foundations of IUCN were laid. After another conference at Brunnen in 1947, the year in which shattered Poland bravely declared the Bialowieza Forest a national park and started to save the European bison, the new Union was formally founded in 1948 at Fontainbleau, France, Huxley, as Director-General of UNESCO, played a key part in all this. Named at first the International Union for the Protection of Nature (IUPN), it had the Swiss Charles Bernard as its first President, and headquarters in Brussels, where it built upon the foundations of the moribund IOPN; in 1961 it moved to Morges in Switzerland, on the shores of the Lake of Geneva.

The new body had two important features. First, governments as well as what are nowadays called NGO's (non-governmental organisations) could be members, and although for some years rather few governments actually joined, today there are 48. Second, the enthusiasm of individual conservationists throughout the world was mobilised and their advice directed on to current problems through the Union's commission system. For most of its existence IUCN (for at its Edinburgh General Assembly in 1956 it changed its name to International Union for Conservation of Nature and Natural Resources) has had five main commissions, dealing with national parks, endangered species, ecology, education, law and, more recently a sixth for environmental planning. The two most important and active of these have been the International Commission on National Parks (recently renamed Commission on National Parks and Protected Areas), whose key role was mentioned in the last chapter, and the Survival Service Commission founded in 1949, whose remit has covered endangered species. For most of its existence the SSC has been especially closely connected with the FPS, for its chairman from 1958 to 1963 was Lt Col C.L. Boyle, Hon. Secretary of the FPS, and since 1963 the chair has been occupied by Sir Peter Scott, who for most of that period was also Chairman of FPS. Since 1963 the present Hon. Secretary of the Society has also played a leading part in the activities of the SSC, latterly as Convener of its Steering Committee. In 1978 the SSC is developing a new, project-oriented programme, under the name of Action Programme Against Extinction (APX).

For most of the 1950s IUCN operated in a comparatively low key, but the Union played a large part in the launching in 1959 of the Charles Darwin Foundation for the Galapagos Islands (CDF) in order to establish a research station in the islands and to provide a continuing scientific presence to watch over one of the most precious ecosystems known to world science. This was most successfully achieved and the Charles Darwin Research Station (CDRS) continues to perform a most valuable function, working closely with the Ecuadorian national parks authorities. Julian Huxley, an FPS Vice-President, was prominently concerned with CDF's foundation and its present Secretary, G.T. Corley Smith is a member of the FPS Council. But, despite its success the difficulties inherent in establishing an internationally controlled organisation on the territory of a developing nation in the last quarter of the 20th century makes it improbable that this model will ever be used again in this precise form. The FPS has made a number of grants to the CDRS, notably for its breeding programme to save the various subspecies of the Galapagos giant tortoise, and in 1978 this programme has just chalked up one of its most notable successes in the saving of the Hood (Espanola) tortoise from almost certain extinction. FPS has also grant-aided the study of the impact of tourism on wildlife in the Galapagos.

IUCN really began to assume its present stature when it promoted, jointly with the UN Food and Agriculture Organisation (FAO), the Africal Special Project. One of the main energisers of this was Dr (now Sir) Frank Fraser Darling, a Vice-President of FPS. The ASP was launched at a conference held at Arusha, Tanzania, in 1961, followed by missions to 17 mostly newly independent African countries; it successfully strengthened both the understanding and the actions of their governments in the early 1960s, which, it was widely feared, would not give adequate priority to the conservation of their wildlife resources. (In many countries these fears proved unfounded.) The African initiative was followed by similar conferences for South-east Asia at Bangkok, Thailand, in 1965, and for Latin America at San Carlos de Bariloche, Argentina, in 1968, both less effective because of their very limited follow-up. IUCN received a further fillip from the United Nations Conference on the Environment at Stockholm in 1972, which led to the creation of the UN Environment Programme, headquartered at Nairobi. UNEP has become an important source of funds for IUCN, and it is at UNEP's request that IUCN has just produced its monumental World Conservation Strategy. In addition to this, IUCN is currently engaged in producing programmes of conservation projects for South-east Asia (already published), Africa south of the Sahara, and Latin America, together with a critical review of the parks and reserves systems of northern and western Europe.

Finance was a problem for IUCN from the beginning, and a main reason for its low-key start during the 1950s. By the early 1960s it was so clear that this was hampering the Union's potential development that a group in which Julian Huxley, Max Nicholson and Peter Scott were prominent, got together and founded the World Wildlife Fund in the autumn of 1961, with the specific aim of raising funds for international wildlife conservation, and in particular for IUCN. Under its first President, Prince Bernhard of the Netherlands, its two Vice-Presidents, Sir Peter Scott and Luc Hoffmann, and its first Director-General, Fritz Vollmar, WWF has successfully operated through national appeals, of which there are now 27. The FPS has been particularly closely connected with the first to be founded, the British National Appeal, recently renamed WWF United Kingdom; over most of the latter's existence between three and six FPS officers or council members have served as trustees of the BNA.

WWF's greatest early achievement was to save Coto Doñana, the famous wildlife reserve at the mouth of the River Guadalquivir in south-western Spain. More recently it has chalked up a considerable success with Operation Tiger, which has so far raised $1,750,000 to help save a species whose numbers in India have fallen below 2000. Great credit is also due to the Indian Government, which set up nine special reserves with the aid of funds contributed by WWF, besides contributing heavily itself, and to other South-east Asian governments for their cooperation. More recently WWF campaigns have been directed towards tropical rain forests, which are being devastated at a catastrophic rate, and marine habitats, whose integrity is currently subjected to innumerable direct and indirect threats. When DDT can be found in the fat of Antarctic penguins, no habitat on earth can be considered safe.

Over the 17 years of its existence WWF has raised a substantial sum of money and has been able to spend over £15m on nearly 2000 projects world-wide. But in the field of wildlife conservation there is never enough money to do all that needs to be done. Ultimately, it is clear, we shall lose the whole game if governments cannot be persuaded to take on most of the burden.

6 | Birds Lead the Way

Throughout the history of wildlife protection, both national and international, there has been a tendency, regretted by most conservationists, for birds to become separated from the rest of the Animal Kingdom. Birds have always been the most popular animal group and so have led the way. Both in Britain and internationally the first stirrings of this special concern for birds began in the late 1860s, when Canon Tristram and Alfred Newton referred to the desirability of protecting birds of prey and seabirds at meetings of the British Association for the Advancement of Science. Almost simultaneously a meeting of German agriculturists and foresters at Vienna in 1868 asked for international agreement to protect animals useful to agriculture and forestry. At this time shooting gulls and other seabirds was a popular pastime. Boats would be hired to convey intrepid sportsmen to the foot of the cliffs at Flamborough Head in Yorkshire, where they could blaze away at nesting guillemots and kittiwakes, and the Thames bridges in London were made hazardous to passers-by whenever hard weather drove the gulls so far up the estuary. So it happened that the first non-game bird protection act in Britain was passed in 1869 to protect seabirds from the shooting "cowboys" of the day. This led to the general Bird Protection Act of 1880, and in due course to the early activities of the Society for the Protection of Birds.

The other strand that led up to the foundation of the SPB in 1889 was an international one, the destruction of thousands of egrets, birds of paradise and even hummingbirds for the millinery trade. Newton again made the running, with a letter in *The Times* in 1876, and this eventually resulted in the formation by Lady Mount Temple of the Plumage League in 1885. The prime aim of the SPB, four years later, was to stop "the enormous destruction of bird life by milliners and others for purely decorative purposes". Among the early supporters, besides Newton, we find the names of Sir Edward Grey and Philip Lutley Sclater, both in attendance at the birth of the SPWFE fourteen years later, as well as Lord Lilford, W.H. Hudson and J.A. Harvie-Brown. Major Stanley Flower, another early SPWFE, pioneered the protection of the egrets of Lower Egypt. He saved the colony, down to 40 pairs, by organising watchers.

Protection of the rarer British breeding birds in the field pre-dated the SPB, for an appeal for funds for the preservation of seabirds in the Farne Islands off the coast of Northumberland had already been launched, and by 1894 there were small local associations in various parts of the country that paid watchers at certain locations during the breeding season. This work was taken up by the SPB, under its Watchers Committee, which for many years used watchers at various sites and ultimately ran the great chain of bird sanctuaries and reserves of its own which the (now Royal) Society for the Protection of Birds built up over the years. The RSPB continued to operate on a fairly small, and often rather select scale for many years, and did not start the membership explosion which led to its present dominating position in the British domestic wildlife conservation scene until well after World War II. Today it has some quarter of a million members, and has with relative ease raised £1 million by public appeal. Largely because of the existence of the RSPB, the FPS has never paid a great deal of attention to British birds, its ornithological interests being mainly confined to its membership of the British Section of the International Council for Bird Preservation. Its Oryx 100% Fund is, however, still the only British source of funds for small overseas bird conservation projects.

After its first airing at Vienna in 1868, the cause of international bird protection was next raised at the First International Ornithological Congress (IOC), also at Vienna, in 1884. It took two more Congresses before the convention to protect birds useful to agriculture was actually signed, by a dozen European countries, not including the United Kingdom, in 1902. Still there was no international organisation of any kind, apart from the quadrennial interest displayed at the IOCs, until 1910, when the 5th Congress at Berlin set up a standing international committee for bird preservation to report to the next Congress, which in the event was not held until 1926. The next impulse came from across the Atlantic, from Dr Gilbert Pearson, President of the National Association of Audubon Societies, which from their earliest days had had a heavy emphasis on birds. After an extensive tour of Europe, Pearson was struck by the general ignorance of ornithologists about what was being done in other countries, so, at a meeting in London on June 20, 1922, he proposed the formation of an International Committee for Bird Preservation. Among those who agreed were P.G. van Tienhoven from the Netherlands, Jean Delacour from France (the only survivor to the present day), Lord Grey of Fallodon, William Lutley Sclater and Frank E. Lemon, whose wife was the stalwart of the RSPB from 1892 to 1943. Grey and Sclater's father had similarly midwifed the SPB and the SPWFE.

The basis of the ICBP, which later changed its name to the International Council for Bird Preservation, was the establishment of national sections, composed not only of bird protection societies, but also including a wide range of complementary interests, such as scientists, sportsmen and faunal conservationists, so that the SPFE became a member of the British Section in 1935. Two important activities of the ICBP have been its concern for the preservation of wildfowl and its fight against the pollution of the sea by oil. Beginning with an initiative by Professor Einar Lönnberg of Sweden in 1935 and spurred on by the Wildfowl Inquiry Committee set up by the British Section in 1935, the movement to protect stocks of ducks, geese, and swans soon became international, and resulted in the creation in 1947 of the International Wildlife Research Institute (later Bureau), currently located at the headquarters of the Wildfowl Trust at Slimbridge, on the Severn estuary in Gloucestershire. The Wildfowl Trust itself, founded by Sir Peter Scott as the Severn Wildfowl Trust in 1948, has played a vital part in securing international action and had a major role in saving at least one species, the nene goose from extinction. Thanks to the genius for public relations displayed by its founder and to his unique talents for melding the scientific, technical and artistic aspects of wildlife conservation to help conserve his special love, the waterfowl, the Wildfowl Trust was the first and most successful of the postwar organisations in Britain devoted to the conservation of individual species or groups of species. Ducks, geese and swans lend themselves especially to a public educational display, and the site chosen, on the Severn estuary, enabled a wild population of white-fronted and other geese also to be shown to the public, under controlled conditions, in the winter months. Similar trusts were later founded to help conserve pheasants, hawks and otters.

ICBP was founded only about three years after oil began to replace coal as a fuel for ships on a large scale, and in the same year that the Brtish Parliament passed its first Act to prohibit the discharge of waste oil within territorial waters, three miles from the coast. Although oiled birds were by no means unknown even in the 1920s — the writer remembers finding his first guillemot, an oiled one, on the Sussex coast in 1926 — it was not until crude oil was brought to Europe in large quantities after World War II that oil pollution began to threaten seabird populations as well as to offend humanitarian susceptibilities. The British Section of ICBP took the initiative in combating this problem, joining with many other interests — fishermen, yachtsmen, bathers, seaside municipalities — to form the Advisory Committee on Oil Pollution of the Sea (ACOPS), and for many years provided its secretariat. The FPS has been active on this Committee since its inception. ACOPS persuaded the UK Government to summon an international conference in 1954, from which emerged the international convention, which has been the basis of the world-wide fight against oil pollution ever since. Recent evidence suggests that oil pollution is probably responsible for substantial falls in breeding auk populations in the north-east Atlantic during the past thirty years. Puffins especially have suffered badly.

As the international wildlife conservation movement limbers up to enter the last two decades of the 20th century, it becomes more and more questionable whether the bird protectionists can indefinitely stay as much apart from the rest of the movement as they are now if they wish to remain effective. Pressures on habitat, which is being destroyed at a geometrically increasing rate, are such that only a great increase in the existing close collaboration between ICBP, IUCN and WWF, can achieve even a minimal portion of the aims of the three organisations. In 1889 and 1922 it made sense for the birds to go it alone. In 1978 it does not, and fortunately it looks as if this closer collaboration will happen quite soon.

7 | Nature Follows On

It took much longer to organise the conservationists interested in British animals other than birds, and you can search the first six volumes of the SPWFE *Journal* in vain for any reference to British mammals — what do they know of England who only the Empire know? In 1909 Sir Harry Johnston complained in that *Journal* that his proposal to make Achill Island, Co. Mayo, a national park had "perished still-born". It seems doubtful if the Society as such had any impact on the first law protecting a non-game British mammal, the first Grey Seals Act 1914.

It was not until 1912 that, stimulated by the Hon. Charles Rothschild, father of the present Lord Rothschild and that distinguished naturalist the Hon. Miriam Rothschild, the Society for the Promotion of Nature Reserves was founded. Curiously, seeking for an endangered British species for its emblem, the new Society poached on the RSPB's territory to choose the red kite, which ten years earlier had been (erroneously, it is now thought) reported to be down to only five individuals in mid Wales. In fact the two societies' paths have been quite different. The SPNR, like all other conservation bodies, was brought to a halt by World War I, but Rothschild himself carried on,

27

stimulated by the need to protect valuable sites from the wartime food production campaign. In 1915 he produced the first list of proposed national nature reserves for Britain, which he recommended to the Board of Agriculture. The list included quite a number of places which are now national nature reserves — Woodwalton Fen, Huntingdonshire; Cothill Fen, Berkshire; Hickling Broad, Norfolk; and Blean Woods, Kent; others such as Wicken Fen, Cambridgeshire and the Farne Islands, Northumberland, are protected by the National Trust and other bodies; and yet others, such as Adventurers' Fen, Cambridgeshire and the South Lancashire dunes have been wholly or partially destroyed.

After the war the SPNR continued in rather a low key, looking somewhat perfunctorily after a handful of reserves it had acquired, and indeed doing very little, even when Rothschild made it a munificent donation of £50,000, a sum which would in those days have purchased land that would now cost well over half a million pounds. Indeed its main *raison d'être* appeared to be a sumptuous annual luncheon for a favoured few out of its deliberately small membership — it was almost a club, and had no membership subscription. More was achieved in the single county of Norfolk between the wars, thanks to the foundation of the Norfolk Naturalists Trust in 1926, largely at the instance of Dr Sidney Long. For twenty years, World War II intervening, no other county took up the challenge, but in 1946 Yorkshire, and two years later neighbouring Lincolnshire, followed suit. After another pause, the appearance of trusts in Leicestershire and Cambridgeshire in 1956 heralded a sudden burst of activity that within another eight years had covered the whole of England and Wales with county naturalists' trusts, now more often called trusts for nature conservation, together with the Scottish Wildlife Trust for the whole of Scotland. This grassroots activity at last stirred up the somnolent SPNR, which placed itself at the head of the county trusts, and under the leadership of Christopher Cadbury from Worcestershire and A.E. Smith from Lincolnshire provided an umbrella under which this growing movement could develop. Today SPNR has changed its name to the Society for the Promotion of Nature Conservation, and has in effect been taken over by the trusts, who themselves constitute its governing body. In 1978 the trusts between then own, lease or manage 1072 nature reserves, covering some 37,000 hectares, and have a combined individual membership of approximately 112,000. This is an achievement hardly to be matched in any other country in the world. The appearance of SPNR made it unnecessary for SPFE to enter the field of domestic conservation, and not until the 1950s did it seriously begin to take up the cudgels on behalf of British mammals, reptiles and amphibians, which lacked any other champion. The FPS still maintains its links with the SPNC through the latter's Conservation

Liaison Committee, an invaluable body which brings together all the major wildlife conservation interests in Britain, both official and unofficial.

Thanks to Norfolk, wildlife conservation in Britain began to be organised locally long before it was organised nationally. For a quarter of a century no official body followed Charles Rothschild's pioneer list of nature reserves; there was just no point in Whitehall which would admit the need to do anything about it. However, the urge for post-war reconstruction which arose quite early in World War II, much to the annoyance of the Prime Minister, provided the opportunity, not only for revising and strengthening the list, but also for devising machinery whereby a system of national nature reserves could be administered. The SPNR took on the task of revising the list of proposed reserves, county by county. It set up a series of county committees, which it foolishly allowed to disappear afterwards, instead of developing them as embryo county trusts. These committees, despite the difficulties of wartime travel, produced what was, until the appearance of the 1977 *Nature Conservation Review*, the nearest approach we have to a Domesday Book of ecologically important sites in England and Wales. The task of devising the administrative machinery both for the national nature reserve system and for an official ecological advice centre, was successfully tackled by the British Ecological Society. It was the Government's appointment of a Wild Life Conservation Special Committee chaired by Julian Huxley, later to be a Vice-President of FPS, that brought together these two documents and gave them an official cachet. The WLCSC was attached to the Hobhouse Committee on National Parks, of which Huxley was a member, and had the present writer as its very junior secretary. The Huxley Committee duly did what was expected of it, and published in 1947 a report which recommended the creation of a Biological Service to administer a series of 73 national nature reserves, largely based on the SPNR list and containing many of the old Rothschild areas too. In the heady atmosphere of radical change in the mid 1940s this recommendation was successfully carried through Parliament in 1949, and the Nature Conservancy was born as an independent Research Council under the Privy Council, with Captain Cyril Diver as its first Dirctor-General. The whole operation was carefully planned and credit is due especially to four individuals, located at various levels in and outside the government machine: Professor A.G. (later Sir Arthur) Tansley, of the British Ecological Society, who together with Captain Diver masterminded the WLCSC Report, Sir John Fryer, Secretary of the Agricultural Research Council, and Max Nicholson, then Secretary to the Lord President's Department. The result was to give Britain a unique piece of machinery, in which the research and administrative sides were melded together in a way that neither was then, nor is now, found in any other part of Whitehall. But the Whitehall machine could not stomach such flouting of its *idée fixe* about the need to separate science and administration, so that in later years the Nature Conservancy was first demoted from its independent position and made a part of the Natural Environment Research Council, and then had its research side taken away and set up as the Institute of Terrestrial Ecology under NERC. The Conservancy itself, renamed the Nature Conservancy Council, was hived off, along with its array of 161 national nature reserves, to an independent position within the Department of the Environment.

Through all its vicissitudes, however, whether as NC or as NCC, the brainchild of Tansley and the British Ecological Society's wartime committee has steadily, against odds, pioneered the sensible application of ecological knowledge to public affairs. For this is the great change that is coming about in politics, both at home and abroad. The dangers of an exploding world population, an accelerating destruction of natural ecosystems, and a consequent steady erosion of natural resources available to feed, clothe and house those burgeoning populations, are becoming apparent even to politicians and administrators. Thanks to the foresight of private conservationists, and precious little thanks to career civil servants or ministers, Britain has a tried and established piece of machinery to funnel ecological advice into policy decisions. Nobody would deny that we still have a long way to go, but in this field Britain did have a head start over the rest of the world.

8 | Ivory and Apes and Egrets

One important strand of the modern wildlife conservation movement began as a protest against the excesses of traders. In the 1880s it was the reaction against the excesses if the plumage trade, notably the pillaging of egret colonies for "osprey" feathers that led to both the RSPB in Britain and to the National Audubon Society (NAS) in the United States. Indeed one of the most famous incidents of the early days was the murder of Warden Guy Bradley by a plume hunter at an egret sanctuary in Florida on July 8, 1905. Great battles were fought, especially in the first thirty years of the century, to secure legislation, both national and international, to restrict the commercial sale of such plumes as egret and bird of paradise, and even as late as 1969 the British Section of ICBP successfully pressed the Government to ban the import of feathers of the endangered grey jungle-fowl, coveted by anglers for their flies. This case was in fact quite a breakthrough, for it proved that the British Government did in fact have powers to ban the import of individual animal products, and thus enabled conservationists later to secure an import ban on whale products.

Ivory was another animal import that quite soon came to need regulation. In 1921 we find the Chairman and Vice-Chairman of the SPFE at the Colonial Office, calling for the implementation of an international convention on the sale of ivory, agreed to before the war, but never signed. South Africa, it was said, did not want to be included, but in the next year we read that General Smuts had assured the Society of his Government's support for an international agreement to restrict the export of ivory below a certain weight. In 1928 everybody was still just talking about the need to control the ivory trade and little but talk happened thereafter. By the late 1970s however, a real crisis has been created for both African and Asian elephants by the virtual conversion of ivory into a currency, which in 1976 accounted for the slaughter of between 100,000 and 400,000 African elephants alone. This unlooked-for effect of the world inflation and depression that followed the oil-price hike of 1973, is currently being vigorously tackled by the IUCN TRAFFIC Group.

In 1927 there is a complaint in the SPFE *Journal* that "the quickest and most certain way of wiping animals off the face of the earth is to commercialise their trophies. That was tried some time ago in Kenya in connection with zebra. It was found that there was quite a good export trade for zebra hides". It has taken fifty years to fulfil this prophecy, but in 1978 there is a real prospect that commercial sales of zebra hides, many of them poached, will exterminate Grevy's zebra and will gravely threaten even the once abundant Burchell's zebra, if it is not controlled.

As early as 1929 we get the first murmurs of the illicit orang-utan trade, which, until it was superseded by the destruction of the rain forest in Borneo and Sumatra, was the main threat to the existence of the largest Asian ape. In that year the Government of the Netherlands East Indies (now Indonesia) asked the British High Commissioner of the Straits Settlements and Federated Malay States (now Malaysia), to prohibit the import of orang-utans into British controlled ports from Dutch controlled territories. After World War II the orang-utan had the misfortune to become a status symbol in South-east Asia, and many high civil and military officials kept illegally taken young orang-utans as pets. Barbara Harrisson started the whole movement for rehabilitation centres for great apes by caring for confiscated illegal young orangs at her home in Sarawak. She and her husband Tom Harrisson then persuaded IUCN to set up the Orang-utan Recovery Service to provide an outlet for confiscated animals that avoided all trade channels. The orangs were passed on to reputable zoos, which had subscribed to the scheme, but without any guarantee that they would actually get one.

Although 23,000 leopard skins were marketed world-wide as early as 1928, adverse trade effects on spotted cats are not reported in the SPFE *Journal* till 1948, when it was reported that Uganda had had to take steps to protect leopards "which have been killed in great numbers owing to the demand for their skins, which command very high prices". The demand grew, till at the Nairobi meeting of IUCN in 1963, the alarming figures of leopard decline in Kenya provided by the Chief Game Warden, Ian Grimwood, led the SSC to put out a statement urging international control. This was one of many strands that led, first to British and later to international measures to restrict trade in endangered species. At one time IUCN had an agreement with the International Fur Trade Association on this subject. The British law, the Animals (Restriction of Importation) Act, 1964, in fact arose from the resolution at the previous IUCN meeting, at Warsaw in 1960. This was pursued vigorously, and at first almost single-handedly by the FPS Secretary, Lt. Col. C.L. Boyle, and finally passed through Parliament under sponsorship of Miss Harvie Anderson, MP. Known among conservationists as "Boyle's law", this Act protected an, at first, fairly restricted list of endangered mammals and reptiles, such as the great apes and the giant tortoises and iguanas of the Galapagos Islands. Birds continued to be dealt with under the Bird Protection Acts. It was administered with the advice of an Advisory Committee, on which several leading members of the FPS served, and was the precursor of the present Endangered Species Act, passed in 1976.

Meantime, IUCN was pursuing its own resolution internationally, but it was more than a dozen years before an international conference actually assembled, at Washington DC, in February 1973, to hammer out a convention on trade in endangered species, of both fauna and flora, which came into force in 1976, and which by April 1978 44 nations had ratified. Both at Washington, and at the later conferences at Berne and Geneva in 1976 and 1977, the FPS has been closely involved both directly and because two of its officers have also represented the SSC. The Convention meant that the British Government had to revise its own legislation, and the resulting Act of 1976 set up a new Scientific Authority for Animals (this time including birds and all other animals), on which several Council members of FPS have continued to serve in their individual capacities. The net effect of all this activity has been greatly to restrict the opportunities that illegal traders have of passing their booty off in the developed countries, while Third World countries have been provided with an instrument to help them to enforce their existing legislation. Even so the United

Kingdom imported the skins of more than 20,000 wild felines in 1976, because some of them are still on Appendix II of the Convention. There are now, however, so many endangered species on the Convention's schedules, including even a few insects and molluscs, that the whole process is in some danger of foundering in its own unwieldiness. Unless the other parties quite soon agree to the simpler British system of protecting everything, except certain listed common and domesticated species, there is good reason to fear that the machinery will break down.

Besides masterminding the whole operation, IUCN has recently created an invaluable instrument for collecting information on international trade in animals and plants. This is its TRAFFIC (Trade Records Analysis of Flora and Fauna in Commerce) Group, under the SSC, which has had especially close links with the FPS, as its Chairman, John A. Burton, is also the Society's Executive Secretary. In its first year's operations, FPS both grant-aided TRAFFIC and gave it house room, and continues to provide the adminsitrative back-up for TRAFFIC's five-man full-time secretariat. TRAFFIC now has a world-wide network of informants, most of them either SSC members or group members, or FPS honorary overseas consultants.

9 | Rake's Progress of the Whalers

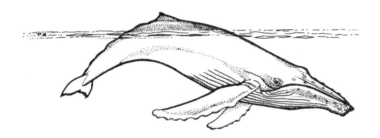

Man's exploitation of fish and marine mammals is a sorry tale of greed and short-sightedness. Some exploiters have paid lip service to the need to conserve stocks. Very few have actually conserved any stocks. Since the English and the Basques wiped out the North Atlantic right whale in the Bay of Biscay in the late Middle Ages and early modern period, stock after stock of whale, seal and fish has been systematically destroyed by overfishing. One of the worst recent examples was the almost deliberate destruction of the haddock fishery off George's Bank, New England, by Russian fishermen using intensive box-fishing techniques. They drove up a steady catch of 50,000 tonnes a year to 150,000 tonnes in 1966; by 1974 the catch was down to 10,000, with nobody benefiting except the Russian consumer in the very short term. Pre-capitalist, capitalist, socialist, communist, all exploit natural populations to the limit if they get the chance.

When the SPWFE came into existence the worst sufferers had been the Atlantic whales and the subantarctic seals. Indeed the southern fur seal has had the melancholy distinction of being commercially wiped out three times over, first in the 1820s, again fifty years later, and once more in the early 1920s. Today it has made a widespread recovery in South Georgia and on many other subantarctic islands, on most of which it is fortunately protected. It was in the early 1920s that the first warning against the depletion of the Antarctic whale stocks appeared in the Society's *Journal*, and it is perfectly clear that from that day to this the whaling industry has set about exploiting the whale stocks to the full, knowing quite well what it was doing. In an all too topical way, the Society complained in 1929 that "It is quite a human trait to 'kill the goose that lays the golden eggs' and doubtless only when the last whale has disappeared will tardy legislation at length emerge".

In 1931 we read of 35 ships and floating factories setting out southwards from Hobart, Tasmania, most of them Norwegian-owned and almost all Norwegian-manned. The Norwegians somewhat disingenuously explained that they had had to come south because there were no more whales left in the Arctic. Six years later the size of the floating factories had greatly increased, and so had the catches of whales. The comment was: "all previous whaling industries have declined and died through overfishing". No wonder a whaling conference had to be held in London in 1938, and agreed to establish the whole Arctic Ocean as a sanctuary and to establish another sanctuary in the Antarctic, and to institute a moratorium (only nobody used that wicked word) on the taking of humpbacks for one year.

No prophecies have been more amply and dismally fulfilled than those relating to the stocks of whales, and although the International Whaling Commission was set up in 1948 specifically to regulate the catching of the great whales, what it has actually done is to preside over a slight slowing down of the process of extinction. One after another the species of great whale have had to be protected absolutely, even by the IWC: all three right whales, gray whale, humpback, blue and now (except in one small area) even the fin whale; year after year the quotas have grown smaller and even those have rarely been fulfilled. It is also significant that one after the other the whaling countries that set up the IWC have withdrawn from the Antarctic pelagic whaling: Britain, New Zealand, the Netherlands, South Africa, Norway. Now South Africa and Australia have closed their land stations. Even Russia and Japan have steadily reduced the size of the fleets they sent down below the Equator. No crystal ball is needed to forecast that the Antarctic whale fishery, which even ten years ago could have been saved as a valuable resource for mankind, will become economically unviable within the next five years.

The FPS, as we have seen, has always taken a close interest in the fate of the great whales, and for the past fifteen years has been represented by an observer at the meetings of the IWC, joining with WWF, the Friends of the Earth and other bodies in attempting, usually fruitlessly, to exercise pressure on the IWC. The concessions that have been made, such as calculating stocks of individual species by area instead of globally, have usually come too late to make any impact. For a long time the great battle was to get the Commission to take any notice of its scientists at all. In the 1960s their advice was regularly ignored if it did not suit the plans of the whaling nations, and even when it was taken one or more whaling nations would use the escape hatch of the "90-day rule" to wriggle out of its obligation to observe a particular quota. In the light of this, it is not surprising that the IWC has always refused to adopt, and often even to consider, the 10-year moratorium that was almost unanimously adopted (by most of the same nations) at the UN Conference on the Environment at Stockholm in 1972, although year by year, as the stocks steadily diminish, the case for it gets stronger. It has, of course, always been supported by FPS, IUCN and WWF. As the SPFE predicted in 1929, it will come only when the last whale has, economically speaking, disappeared.

Seal fisheries have followed the same rake's progress as whale fisheries, and many stocks have been wiped out over the years, or at any rate reduced to a size when it no longer pays to harvest them. Just before World War I the grey seal stocks of the British Isles were brought to so low an ebb (there has always been a great dispute as to the actual figures) that the British Parliament was moved to introduce a close season, in what for many years remained the only British law protecting a non-game mammal. The inadequacy of this law and its successor in 1932 was a considerable bone of contention, only resolved when a new one, the Conservation of Seals Act, was passed in 1970, as a result of a meeting in the FPS office, on the Society's initiative. The Act was guided through parliament by the Earl of Cranbrook, a Council member and later a Vice-President of the Society. It protected not only the grey, but for the first time the common seal, some populations of which, for instance in the Shetlands and the Wash, had been at risk from uncontrolled shooting. It was the first genuine conservation measure for a British wild animal, for it made provision for the licensed harvesting of stocks of seals that scientific advice indicated could be safely culled. Thus the British seals have been more fortunate than the whales of the high seas, where no legal writ ran.

There are only four marine mammals, on the world scale, that have been saved by protection; the western stock of the gray whale, which migrates from the Bering Sea to the Pacific coast of Mexico, the Pribilof fur seal and the northern sea otter of the Aleutian islands, and the polar bear. The southern fur seal and southern elephant seal have been saved less by protection than by being left alone to recover and not exploited again, although their protection in the British-controlled subantarctic islands has certainly helped. Unrestricted whaling brought the eastern gray whale near to extinction between 1840 and the 1920s, since when it has been protected and has recovered to about 12,000. The Pribilof fur seal of the far North Pacific provides one of the classic stories of near-extermination by unbridled exploitation. Even as early as 1805 the Russian Government imposed a two-year moratorium in a vain attempt to save the stocks near their coasts. Not till 1911, when the stocks had fallen to 200,000, only 8 per cent of their original size, did the sealing nations come together and hand the care of the stocks over to the United States, which has managed them so well that there are now more than a million and a half again. This has enabled the resumption of harvesting on a controlled basis, so that the Pribilof fur seal shows what can be done if only conservation commonsense is allowed to prevail. At about the same time that the US was starting to save the Pribilof seal, it also took in hand the sea otter, whose valuable fur led it to a similar disaster at the hands of Russian and American hunters. The sea otter also has been built up again, and several thousand inhabit various Aleutian islands. Here too a small experimental harvest has been started again, but otters are not so prolific as seals and it will take a good many more years really to repair the damage done by the free-for-all in earlier years.

10 | From the Dodo to the Koala

In the century before the SPWFE was founded 18 species of mammal became extinct: best known are the quagga of South Africa, extinct about 1878, the sea mink of North America (c 1880) and the Antarctic wolf of the Falkland Islands (1876). Only a few years outside this period too come another South African animal, the blaaubok, believed to have been exterminated by 1800 and Steller's sea cow, discovered in 1741 and extinct by 1768. The problem of endangered species therefore existed already, but not in acute form it does today, and the founders of the Society wisely concentrated at first on protecting commoner species, to prevent them reaching the zone of endangerment. Since that date some twenty full species and 14 subspecies of mammal have been reported as extinct, though several have been rediscovered. The almost certainly extinct species are mostly marsupials, bats or rodents, there being some doubt about the actual extinction of such better known species as the thylacine of Tasmania, the Caribbean monk seal, Przewalski's horse and the Arabian oryx. The supposedly extinct species which were later rediscovered include the parma wallaby, the bridled nail-tailed wallaby, and Leadbeater's possum, indicating how little Australian zoologists really know about their huge country, the yellow-tailed woolly monkey of Peru and the hispid hare and pygmy hog of northern India. Among subspecies the Bali race of tiger is the most noteworthy of those that probably really is now extinct, while the Mexican race of the grizzly bear has the melancholy distinction of having become "probably extinct" twice in the past twenty years.

Attention began to be focussed on endangered species during World War II, with the publication of two important volumes by the American Committee for International Wild Life Protection, under the aegis of the New York Zoological Society. These were *Extinct and Vanishing Mammals of the Western Hemisphere*, by G.M. Allen (1942) and the corresponding volume for the Old World, by Francis Harper (1945). They were followed by *Extinct and Vanishing Birds of the World*, by James C. Greenway (1958). These initiatives stimulated the First Technical Conference of IUCN at Lake Success, in northern New York State, in 1949 to draw up lists of 14 endangered mammals and 13 endangered birds, for immediate action. Eleven of these 27 species are the subject of active conservation programmes today: mountain zebra, Javan and great Indian rhinos, European bison, Indian lion, Mediterranean monk seal, nene goose, Laysan duck, whooping crane, cahow and California condor. Most are succeeding, though the cahow and condor population trends still give great cause for concern. One, the North African bubal hartebeest, is definitely extinct, and five others are either feared extinct or have such tiny populations that they are on the edge: Caribbean monk seal, thylacine, Arabian ostrich, pink-headed duck and Eskimo curlew.

Not until Peter Scott became Chairman of the IUCN Survival Service Commission in 1963 did a systematic study of the endangered species problem begin. The Red Data Books (RDB) are his brainchild, and have transformed the study of endangered species, with their detailed information on the status, distribution and conservation problems of each species or subspecies. The first RDB, for mammals, appeared in 1966, and has been followed by volumes on birds, reptiles and amphibians, freshwater fish, and plants. Further volumes on

butterflies and moths and other invertebrates are in prospect. There
are five categories of endangerment:

1. Endangered (printed on red sheets): species or subspecies in
   danger of extinction and whose survival is unlikely if the casual
   factors continue operating.
2. Vulnerable (yellow sheets): species or subspecies believed likely
   to move into the endangered category in the near future if the
   casual factors continue operating.
3. Rare (white sheets): species or subspecies with small world
   populations that are not at present endangered or vulnerable but
   are at risk.
4. Out of Danger (green sheets): species or subspecies formerly
   regarded as endangered, vulnerable or rare, but which are now
   considered relatively secure because effective conservation
   measures have been taken or the previous threat to their survival
   has been removed.
5. Indeterminate (grey sheets): species or subspecies suspected of
   being either endangered, vulnerable or rare, but for which
   existing information is inadequate.

On this basis there are in the RDB Mammals as revised in 1978 sheets
for 150 endangered, 79 vulnerable, 52 rare, 34 indeterminate and 6 out
of danger species or subspecies. The RDB's have established
themselves as essentials tools for the conservation of endangered
species, especially in connection with the Washington Convention on
International Trade in Endangered Species of Fauna and Flora. Indeed
they rank as one of IUCN's major achievements, and to the general
public are probably the best known aspect of the Union's work. FPS
has been particularly closely connected with the latest phase of the
revision of the RDB Mammals, as its Hon. Secretary is Chairman of the
Advisory Panel and the compiler, Jane Thornback, works in the FPS
Office, using FPS facilities.

Over the years FPS has been concerned, directly or through its
officers, with many individual endangered species, notably the white
rhinoceros, the koala, Père David's deer and the Arabian oryx, the last
two by means of captive breeding. The white or square-lipped
rhinoceros, the largest land mammal after the elephants, was once
widespread and abundant in southern Africa, but by the end of the
19th century slaughter by both Boers and British had reduced the
southern race to a tiny remnant, discovered in 1894 near the junction of
the Black and White Umfolozi Rivers in Zululand. Even here,
according to Frederick Selous, six were shot in that year. The Umfolozi
Game Reserve was created in 1894 for their benefit, but seems to have
been remarkably ineffective at first. As late as 1929 we find a
complaint in the SPFE *Journal* that only twenty of the southern race of

the white rhino survived in the world, all in Umfolozi, and that three of these had been illegally killed in 1928. It was actually proposed to abolish the game reserve. Fortunately in 1930 the decision was reversed. Within five years the rhinos had begun to spread into the nearby Hluhluwe reserve, and by 1945 there were 250-300 rhinos in the two reserves and the situation was saved. Then during the next fifteen years the pendulum swung the other way; effective conservation measures produced such a population explosion that overgrazing endangered the habitat. By 1960, with some 800 rhinos all told, 730 of them in Umfolozi, it was urgently necessary to remove some. Since then several hundred rhinos have been immobilised and translocated, at first mainly to other African game parks but latterly also to many reputable zoos and safari parks all over the world, including 30 to the Zoological Society of London's Whipsnade Park. The FPS grant-aided one of the first of these operations, the removal of a pair to the small Mlilwane reserve in Swaziland. No praise can be too high for the way the Natal Parks Board has tackled these problems, under the guidance first of Colonel Jack Vincent and later of Ian Player. By contrast it is sad to realise that the future of the northern race of the white rhino, found in Sudan, Uganda and Zaire, is far from secure.

The plight of the koala was a constant concern to the Society in its early days, and indeed the koala appears to have been the first land mammal actually saved from extinction in the wild by deliberate conservation measures. Not until the early 1920s were any of the Australian state governments prevailed on to give any form of protection to an animal that was being decimated by hunters for its fur and often left wounded to die by "sportsmen" with a perverted sense of "fun". Queensland, always the most backwoods of the states, relapsed in 1927 and allowed 600,000 skins to be exported. Not surprisingly, by 1939 the koala was extinct in South Australia, and down to 200 in New South Wales, 1000 in Victoria and even in Queensland, where once there had been millions, to 10,000. Fortunately since the war protection has been enforced, there has been an extensive reintroduction programme in Victoria and the animal is widespread in eastern Australia.

11 | *Saved by Captive Breeding*

The history of captive or controlled breeding as a means of saving endangered species dates back to the successful efforts to save the American bison or buffalo at the end of the last century. By 1883, after years of boundless slaughter, only a single genuinely wild herd remained in the United States, outside national parks and refuges. In September of that year a party of hunters set out to kill them all, and by November they had done so. Six years later out of the many millions a century earlier, only 541 bison were known in North America (the Canadian herd in what is now Wood Buffalo Park was undiscovered), all either in captivity or in the Yellowstone National Park, where poaching was rife. It took another five years for Congress to pass a law protecting the bison, and eight more to persuade it to appropriate $15,000 to build up the small Yellowstone herd. In 1905, stimulated by Dr William Hornaday of the New York Zoological Society (NYZS), which had been breeding up a captive stock, the American Bison Society was founded to help build up herds elsewhere, and the NYZS gave fifteen animals to help establish a free-ranging herd in the Wichita Mountains Wildlife Refuge in Oklahoma. Today, with well over 10,000 in various parts of the United States alone, the bison is saved, largely because national parks and wildlife reserves existed to which zoo-bred animals could quickly be moved.

The problem with the next animal to be tackled in this way was that it has no known wild habitat, although it is believed to have formerly inhabited marshlands. The mi-lu or Père David's deer became known to western science in 1865 when the French explorer-priest Armand David became the first foreigner to see what lay inside the 45-mile wall of the Imperial Hunting Park near Peking. This curious donkey-like animal may have become extinct in the wild some two or three thousand years ago, but in 1895 it nearly became extinct altogether. In that year a flood breached the park wall, and all but a score escaped and were either drowned or eaten by hungry peasants. In 1900 the foreign troops brought in to quell the Boxer Rebellion also quelled the last remaining stock in the park. In a few years the mi-lu became extinct in China, and if foreign zoos and private collectors had not managed to get a few out, it would have become extinct altogether. At this point the eleventh Duke of Bedford, great-grandfather of the present Duke and President of the SPWFE, stepped in. He persuaded the European zoos to let him collect all the available animals together into his extensive park at Woburn Abbey in Bedfordshire. By 1914 he had built this herd up from 18 to 88, a total reduced to 50 by the end of the war, when he was forbidden to buy extra winter feed for them. However, by the outbreak of World War II he and his successors had raised the total to some 200, and now there are 777 in captivity throughout the world, mainly in zoos. Though the species has been saved, it seems unlikely that it can ever be released into the wild, unless at some future date the Government of China is able to set aside an extensive marshland national park. Even so, it may by then have lost its special adaptation to the marshland. For one of the drawbacks of captive breeding is that the longer the species remains in captivity, the more likely it is that the process of evolution is selecting for life in captivity rather than life in the wild.

Several other species were saved in this way in the years just before and just after World War I. The European bison, or wisent, which has its own special society, the International Society for the Protection of the European Bixon, was saved largely by the Poles, who preserved it in the Bialowieza Forest through the horrors of World War II. Their good work has been carried on by the Russians, who have spread wisent stocks in forests throughout the European part of the USSR, thanks in large degree to the efforts of Professor Andrei Bannikov, a Vice-President of the FPS. The rescue of Przewalski's horse, which may now be actually extinct in the wild, unless a few survive in Inner Mongolia, was very much a zoo job. The first attempts to perpetuate it in captivity were made at the two famous collections at Askaniya Nova in the Ukraine and Woburn Abbey, England, but both eventually died out. The present world captive population of 252 animals originated entirely from two small herds, each about a dozen strong, which survived at the Prague and Munich Zoos in 1950. Two South African ungulates, the bontebok and the Cape mountain zebra were originally preserved from extinction by the action of a handful of Afrikaner families, who carried on the Kruger tradition by keeping them on their ranches. More recently each has had a national park set up on its behalf.

The classic instance of successful captive breeding was Operation Oryx, planned and carried out by the FPS in 1962, with the aid of a substantial grant from the infant WWF, founded the previous year. Alarmed by reports which suggested the imminent extinction of this handsome antelope, coveted by hunting Arabs as a virility symbol, the Society sent an expedition, led by Major Ian Grimwood, Chief Game Warden of Kenya, now an FPS Vice-President, to the extreme eastern portion of what is now South Yemen to capture a small stock. Two males and one female were caught, and sent to Phoenix Zoo in Arizona, where the climate is like that of southern Arabia. Here they were joined by a female loaned by the Zoological Society of London, and later by another female presented to FPS by the Ruler of Kuwait. In the following year four more oryxes came from the Riyadh Zoo, the gift of King Saud of Saudi Arabia to WWF. The trustees of the World Herd of Arabian Oryx are the Arizona Zoological Society, FPS, the Shikar-Safari Club (who helped with the transport costs), WWF (USA) and the Zoological Society of London. This has now proved to be one of the most successful efforts at captive breeding of an endangered species, especially since a number of animals, surplus to Phoenix's capacity, were deposited at San Diego Zoo Wild Animal Park, where they have bred even faster than at Phoenix. There are now 91 animals in the World Herd in addition to 38 belonging to Los Angeles Zoo and 80-90 in private collections in Qatar and elsewhere along the Gulf, and at last, in 1978, a start has been made in the original aim of returning some to Arabia. Four males were airlifted to Amman, Jordan, in February 1978, and it is hoped that females will join them by the end of the year. There is no immediate likelihood that oryxes can be released into the wild in Jordan, because of the danger of poaching across international frontiers, but the Shaumari enclosure, where they now are, is 20 sq.m in extent. In Oman, however, there is a real prospect that within three or four years, some can be released into the wild and guarded by a tribe dedicated to preserving them from the international poachers, who exterminated the oryx in Oman only four years ago. The Arabian oryx may or may not be now extinct in the wild: the FPS hears rumours to the contrary but perhaps it is best that they remain rumours, for the motorised Arab hunters of the oryx are so determined and ruthless that an unguarded wild stock would have no chance of survival.

Some of the most successful captive breeding schemes for endangered species have been for birds, most notably the nene or

Hawaiian goose, which has been especially associated with the name of Sir Peter Scott, founder and energiser of the Wildfowl Trust. From a low point of less than 50 individuals, about 30 in the wild and 13 in captivity, in 1949, the Wildfowl Trust and both public and private efforts in Hawaii itself, have brought numbers up to approximately 2,000, of which 1,250 are in captivity and 750 in the wild. The island of Maui has been largely restocked with Wildfowl Trust birds, and although these have not had the full breeding success that had been hoped for it is a most notable achievement. Two bodies have saved pheasant species from extinction: Gerald Durrell's Jersey Wild Life Preservation Trust with the white-eared pheasant and the Pheasant Trust of Philip Wayre, a member of the FPS Council, which has returned Swinhoe's and cheer pheasants bred in Norfolk to the wild in Taiwan and India respectively, and has also helped to restock Sweden and Western Germany with eagle owls.

The FPS has always been interested in captive breeding as a means of averting species extinction, and has played its part in four conferences held on this subject. The first two were held at London Zoo in 1964 under IUCN auspices and at San Diego, California under San Diego Zoo. The second two were directly promoted by FPS, the first jointly with the Jersey Wild Life Preservation Trust at Jersey Zoo in 1972, the second jointly with the Zoological Society of London at Regent's Park in 1976, as part of the latter's 150th anniversary celebrations. It is hoped to hold the third in the series, jointly with San Diego Zoological Society, at San Diego in 1979.

12 | Looking Forward

At the beginning of the 20th century, with the apocalyptic fate of the American bison ringing in their ears, conservationists thought mainly of setting aside game reserves, places where the hunting of game animals would be controlled. The idea of protecting animals that people did not want to shoot, let alone plants, hardly occurred to anybody. At the end of the century what rings in our ears is not so often a fusillade of shots, as the growl of the bulldozer and the deafening crash of falling timber. It is habitat destruction, even inside national parks and nature reserves, that is our number one problem today. If the Fauna Preservation Society is to have any *raison d'être* at its centenary in 2003, this is the problem it must tackle.

The gravest danger today is to wetlands and tropical rain forests, both highly productive habitats, but the danger to the marine environment from pollution is almost equally great. Two of them have been the subject of recent major fund-raising campaigns by WWF. Rather more than half (935m hectares) of the world's total potential rain forest area is still forest, but it is estimated that within 85 years it will be all gone at present rates of exploitation. In the Ivory Coast for instance, the rain forest is being destroyed at the rate of 400,000 ha every year, and in Laos, Madagascar, and Thailand, at the rate of 300,000 ha. Nigeria now actually has to import timber. Moreover, the destruction of rain forest is usually virtually irreversible. When the trees are gone, the soil is washed away by heavy tropical rainstorms, erosion gullies appear, and flash floods endanger the communities living downstream. Whole deserts, such as the one in Rajputana, western India, have been created by large-scale destruction of rain forests. And the only beneficiaries, and that in the short term, are the consumer countries of the west, and Japan.

Conservationists have hitherto been mainly technologists, experts in particular animals or plants or groups of animals or plants and how they need to be treated to be saved from extinction. In future they must not only be ecologists, for unless they understand ecology they are whistling in the wind, but also politicians, for the task they have to tackle is basically a political one. The accelerating destruction of the world environment has gone beyond the stage where small numbers of dedicated people organised in private societies can do much to help, except on a quite local scale, such as the county naturalists' trusts in Britain. Only the people of the world can stop the destruction of their environment, so that only by persuading the people of each country that it is in their own interest to pressurise their politicians to conserve renewable natural resources can the world's natural environment be preserved into the 21st century. People who are cold, or hungry, or wretchedly housed want only to get warm, to feed and to house themselves. The first impulse of hungry people who see the vast "empty" areas of national parks, for instance La Macarena in Colombia, the Gunung Leuser in Sumatra, or even the Serengeti in Tanzania, is to move in to hunt or cultivate or settle. Politicians, if they are to be persuaded to stop this must be presented not only with powerful technical arguments, but with the evidence of a strong public opinion among their electorates. Ultimately it comes down to the success of politicians in doing their ordinary job, to ensure the welfare of all their people, for it takes a strong government to withstand the short-term pressures to destroy natural resources in favour of the long-term one for conserving them. The intervention of bodies of foreigners, however august, is liable to get short shrift.

The task for the future thus is to get right back to the grass-roots. We have, of course, to get our technical information right, to be up to date with our facts, to know just how each animal and plant lives, to be able to advise on how to save it. But unless we find some means of getting across to the people of the world the urgent and essential need to preserve the environment they and their children have to live in, we shall in the end lose the whole shooting match.